UNQUIET VIGIL

NEW AND SELECTED POEMS

PAUL QUENON, OCSO

PARACLETE PRESS
BREWSTER, MASSACHUSETTS

2014 First printing

Unquiet Vigil: New and Selected Poems

© 2014 The Abbey of Gethsemani

ISBN: 978-1-61261-560-8

Some of the poems in this collection originally appeared in *Terrors of Paradise*, Black Moss Press, 1996; *Laughter My Purgatory*, Black Moss Press, 2002; *Monkswear*, Fons Vitae, 2008; *Afternoons with Emily*, Black Moss Press, 2011; and *Bells of the Hours*, Fons Vitae, 2014. They are reprinted by permission.

The Paraclete Press name and logo (dove on cross) is a trademark of Paraclete Press, Inc.

Library of Congress Cataloging-in-Publication Data
Quenon, Paul.
  [Poems. Selections]
  Unquiet vigil : new and selected poems / Paul Quenon.
    pages cm. — (Paraclete poetry)
  Summary: "What might briefly tumble through a monks mind, or be hard chiseled over a span of years, what might be gleaned while ranging high along the Kentucky knobs, or what quietly emerges while sitting in the dark before dawn-these are the inner and outer landscapes of the religious poems found in Unquiet Vigils. From nocturnal Vigils to close listening to the liturgy of crickets, these are litanies of love and life, work, patience, and prayer. These poems are collected from over two decades of writing, and seasoned with the savor of five decades of living a monastic life. "— Provided by publisher.
  ISBN 978-1-61261-560-8 (paperback)
  I. Title.
  PR9199.3.Q45A6   811'.54—dc23
  2014018909

10 9 8 7 6 5 4 3 2 1

Published by Paraclete Press
Brewster, Massachusetts
www.paracletepress.com

Printed in the United States of America

CONTENTS

AUTHOR'S NOTE

To keep vigil is literally to watch.
"Watch" is that one-word command given us by Jesus,
much like the one word that opens the Holy Rule of St.
Benedict: "Listen." The monastic life is a lifelong practice
of both watching and listening. After fifty-five years at this
I am still a beginner. My vigils are difficult, my listening
partial. Unquiet comes into the vigil from many sides,
but primarily from myself—from not doing what are the
easiest of commands: Watch. Listen. They are one and the
same thing really, but I am many and divided.

These poems are a circling around silence to see and
watch what is heard, a use of words to fix in hearing what is
not quite seen. Writing has been for me, in a broad sense,
a way of vigil-keeping, of making the watch something
more of my own. I have not made writing my primary
purpose in life; it is a means of enhancing my monastic
vocation, and that is primary. But it also flows out of the
wellspring of contemplative life lived every day.

Not every monk writes, but when I do it is from a middle
ground between being an individual person and being a

monk who lives in community. That middle ground is the soil from which these poems spring. Inevitably, the man I am makes the poetry I write, but to make the man its primary object does a disservice to poetry. To make poetry out of being a monk does a disservice to the monk. So this poet must make do with straddling the two. God save me from writing as a monk! That makes for bad poetry. And God save me from poetry that is only about the man. It is a bore to everyone, including myself.

This middle span can be an uncharted sea at times and a tight squeeze at others. At its best it is an open arena, a playground where I forget identities and let life speak for itself. Or I let death speak, or circumstances, or boredom, or I let freedom speak in the midst of all of these.

My poems have cropped up out of the leisure of a monastic life, busy as that life often can be. I have the luxury of not needing to write to survive, so what goes onto a page is an overflow of the contemplative life, of the regular round of prayer, work, and reading that is the daily fare of a monk. Poetry naturally emerges from this context, whether it is written down or not. Writing has the advantage of bringing enhanced attention to what is already in the air and crafts it into a form other people can share. My Novice Master, Fr. Louis (Thomas Merton), once said that a monk should know how to write a good poem. It should be within the range of his contemplative practice. Not that he has to write often, but at least he has a sense of what goes into writing poetry and what it is about.

I was given encouragement early in my novitiate when I showed a poem to Fr. Louis and he posted it on the bulletin board for others to read. Not until fifteen years later, after focusing on philosophy and theology, did I begin writing poetry regularly, and over the next forty years the pace slowly built and publications followed. It always seems surprising to me how moments that seem most personal, specific, and immediate to me can likewise speak to other people.

My latest efforts, the *What-Not Poems*, are partly an effort to get beyond writer's block by writing about it. These poems also make a beginning at coming to terms with the ever-present ending where I stand before the door of the unspoken and can only loiter there as meanings emerge or withhold themselves. Anything what-not might appear, and something like predestination might be involved, given that my French-Belgian name, Quenon, can be roughly translated as "what-not."

The selection of Haiku represents the closest bond for me between meditation and poetry, since I often begin or end a period of silent sitting with a haiku as a kind of punctuation of the chosen moment, such as it might be.

Bells of the Hours derives its inspiration mostly from the monastic ambience and listens closely to the frequent sound of bells that call the community to the hours of the Divine Office. The same bells are always rung, but a careful attention yields variations in overtones and meanings. What does the moment have to say? What is in the air? What is heard in the resonances?

Afternoons with Emily was written under the deep influence of Emily Dickinson regarding style, love of solitude, and nature. She became a steady soul-friend over the years with my daily visits to read or memorize what came from such a monastic kind of heart.

Monkswear is a word-play on the religious habit we wear, and on the fact that monks swear solemn vows. Likewise, every poem is a kind of oath, holy or profane, when it comes from the heart. My writing adviser, Marty Gervais, recommended I write about things close to home. What is closer than the clothes you wear on your back? So that became my focus for a while, and I included each distinctive garment of a monk. There was nothing symbolic or theological in the attempt, only the intention of conveying what it feels like to live inside these garments, and what incidental meanings they casually accumulate over years of use.

Laughter My Purgatory implies that one of the best ways to get clear and free is to laugh at yourself. And sometimes the best purification, the best corrective is to pay attention when others laugh at you. This is a benign kind of purgatory—as is love from the past in the tender recovery of memories of people: twin Sister, Mother, Grandmother, Dad.

Something of paradox is found in *Terrors of Paradise*. Not everything is bliss within the *paradisus claustralia*: there are demons of anxiety, conceit, secretiveness, frustration, boredom—along with the angels of silence, order, wonder, community, and devotion. This volume, my first published poetry, was found by Marty Gervais of Black Moss Press, who has a knack for discovering new talents and giving them a beginning. My continuing thanks go to him, as well as to J. Robert Hill, who often helped on revisions.

Thanks to Gray Henry, with Fons Vitae, who has taken me into her vast fold of Muslim, Buddhist, and Christian writers, for we have joyfully collaborated for decades on interreligious events and exchange. Thanks also for friends who have been reliable readers and advisors: Lynn Szabo, Mike Bever, Michael Lance, Dave Harrity. I greatly appreciate as well the solid support and encouragement of Fenton Johnson, Judith Valente, Nana Lampton, Eleanor Miller, Jonathan Montaldo, Fr. Timothy Kelly, ocso, and Fr. Elias Dietz, ocso.

NEW POEMS

What-Not Poems

GONE MISSING

I

Kindly reader, I am a poem without a poet.
He has gone missing for weeks
and my house is empty. Suffer me awhile,
or go, and if you meet him—
he with a distant look and shambling gait—
tell him the hearth is cooling down.

I won't know a thing for days,
he takes to a walk-about
and never pays me notice.
What kind of life is that?

Yet I've never expected different—
I'm glad he just comes back at all.
And you could say absence
sometimes makes for a better poem.

II

Words eluded me like tall
white tails of winter-grey deer,
ghosts in flight through
trees. Suddenly a poem,
with head, eyes, and ears, stopped,
stared, then disappeared.
So I followed—picked through

iambics overgrown, clambered over
feelings weighted, uprooted, overturned,
and came home with a scent

gone lost, faint recall of ancient
stanzas, patient, noble and tall
where none pass by to hear.

WHAT-NOT POEMS

A what-not comes from nowhere,
never waited to appear.

To air it brings no growth
no weather wears it down.

It never shows ambition
it sits there mute as stone,

a cast off what-not
uncarved block come

from nowhere.

WORDS UNDEAD

When something
separates itself from
the un-said
and stands there inadequate
ridiculous and
said,
you wish
to put it in the attic
and act as it were dead.

IMPATIENT EAR

Robin smartly steps,
pauses, listens long
to the mute ground,
flairs head feathers,
leans closer
then pecks precisely
something there
getting in his way.

He ate it, yes—
what kept him from
listening carefully
most carefully to the mute,
the excellently mute,
ground.

LARK ASCENDING

Not how high he goes it is
but from where he ascended,

where he hid, and whence
he followed his music when
it escaped, and had to catch up with it
just to stay alive.

No sound is so pure—
so pure it can never be possessed
and never can be lost,

even though youth and all it wants to remember
is ground up in mower blades
that surely will come,
come with the blunt, blind, mindless harvester
that music will never stop.

Nor stopped can be the music
as seasons rise again in tall, fertile grass
with bowed, seedy heads full of

pure musings of a lark ascending.

SPECULATING SWALLOWS

Swallows wheel below me
seated high on a windowsill
as I read Rilke this rainy evening.
In chorus they sweep close to me,
curious and much amused at this aerial man
perched two stories up.

They make clipped remarks with swift wing beats
as they sail past my window.

Well—the delight is mutual.

I return to the page and read:
I am! You anxious One, don't You hear me
with my soft senses surging toward You?
My feelings, which have found wings,
circle around Your face innocently.

How strange! How did they know? Am I God to these
swallows?
Or be they God wooing me?

They befriended me briefly in their god-like play,
then passed beyond to loftier freedom.

Prayers of a Young Poet, Rainer Maria Rilke, tr. Mark S. Burrows
(Paraclete Press, Brewster MA, 2013).

LITTLE RASCAL

How is it birds who
come in plain jackets sing so
extravagantly?

Little brown winged-thing,
hardly worth looking at,
urchin hid in shrub,

tell me where you stole
that dazzling necklace
strung with diamond notes?

Out of God's pocket?

TRANSPIRATION

The forest's green brow billows
towards white ranges of cumulus
piling tall—a host towering
over leafy hoards crowding below.
Two solemn masses, two summer throngs
breathing one sunlit worship.

Two transfigurations:
vapor heaving updrafts to evanesce into light;
groundwater exhaling into wind through roiling foliage.

Transubstantiation—that's all
of you and me. We vanish into light—
the untamed, deathless light.

CUBBY HOLE UNDER THE STAIRS

Peace came to my door
without luggage or sandals,
with just its name—peace.

Hungry and cold, peace
asked for nothing but to give
of itself in peace.

My rooms all crowded
with anxiety, I had
little room for peace,

littered with wants,
I cleaned a small space for peace
in a cubby hole

under the staircase
where peace lived very simply,
not asking for much

and we would visit
at odd moments, made odder
for their rarity.

But slowly I learned
to come looking for nothing,
for peace had nothing

but itself to give.

So I grew to live without
expectations, poor

at last at peace.

THE SURFACE OF THINGS

Is everything really illusion?
Might I pass through this heavy oak door
without opening it?

I lean gently to and feel it yield to weight,
swaying in agreement—
my respect for its solidity,
to my passage it yields a breath of concession.

Jesus had such exquisite care
not to disturb the surface of water
that he could walk on it.

CALLING CARD

I sat waiting by the door of my open mind
on the Seniorate patio.
Sunrise came, bird song, in
stirless air fraught with drought.

Where must be—what opens to my openness?

Hope with shortened breath waited,
laid like a doormat seldom crossed.

My attention strayed, faltered and bent to
a black mat, edged toward the corner of my eye,
with the brand name

NOTRAX

trademark as well, you might say,
of One who crossed the Red Sea
 . . . and no one saw his footprints.

begins with No
ends with X

with no vestige left
on my desolate doorstep

at my feet a calling card instead:
Notrax
dropped to say he is already gone.

Oh well, what else would I expect?
until tomorrow then.

Meanwhile,

I hear a faint aluminum crank
as Br. Frederic on a walker
approaches and wordlessly rolls
across the Notrax mat, through the door
as he does daily

respectful of my stirless silence
which lingered behind after Tierce bell rang
and I had departed.

SEVERE MONSTRANCE

Spied through tree lattice
accumulating gold
brims up slow, fierce, blinding;

swells to full treasure,
rounds to a prince of a sun
set on day's swift course.

Severe monstrance mounted,
defying adoration:
eyes pained dash to ground:

none see God and live.

WESTMINSTER ABBEY

I casually browsed the ambulatory,
where kings and dignitaries lie
in tombs plaqued with names
I will never aspire to know.

Suddenly, I was tricked
to alertness by a seated sloppy stone fellow
who seemed more out of place in holy church
than Generals and knights. His was an air
of bonhomie, mischief on
an unglamorous face, puffy,
and subtly lit with a smile—quite like
some quaint tradesman out of Dickens.

The name William Wilberforce stopped me
then spun me back to read clear to the floor,
left me squatting on my heels
—the great emancipationist and Parliamentarian—
I nearly tilted forward onto my knees
before this figure, the first here to provoke worship.
But caught myself, lest this jolly stone man
squirm with embarrassment.

THE UN-NAMED CAT MERTON

A radioactive atom
unobserved
is in a state of decay
and non-decay
at once

In the black box
Schrodinger's cat,
depending for its life
on that unobserved atom,
is in a state
dead and alive
both

Two stone Buddhas at
Polonnaruwa,
the one awake, standing,
the other lies asleep.

Both, when you are *jerked clear*
out of the habitual,
half-tied vision of things
are one Buddha
asleep and awake.

Unpublished photograph
in the locked black box file
of the monastery dark-room:

two monks, one prone
cottonballs blocking nostrils,
another standing by at watch.
Black and white image:

Fr. Louis dead, Dom Leclercq alive
both, one monk,
dead and alive
both

when
unobserved.

I took to calling these eight poems a series of "What-Not Lives."

PUP

I was a pup, and when a stranger would walk by our
house, my mom would go out in the yard and bark at
him. Good Mom!

GROUNDHOG EXTRAORDINAIRE

In my prime I was a groundhog with attitude. I climbed
tiers of a retaining wall and crossed the high gardens
and leisure parks above safety of the level fields where
common groundhogs burrow. In my rich dark coat I
made my way through upper neighborhoods and down
steep escarpments not well suited for rotund gentlemen.
Unlike my kind, I matured with a verve that was forgetful
of the closest run to the ground hole. Others may have
sat up on their haunches to stare at the distance, but I was
gone and found on elevations they only dreamt of.
That was a summer of sun and frequent rains.
We thought it would last forever.

SPARROWS

When I was a sparrow—the Chipping kind—my wife
and I walked along with contentment under the towering
daffodils. Sidewalks were much to our ease and we
tamely strayed not far from strolling monks. They were of
much interest to us—gentle as they were. One or another,
passing, might even talk to us. So we would flit ahead
in the lead with hops, chips, and chirps to keep the tone
alive—especially such moments as when the air filled with
bells and set an urgency into the steps of monks towards
whatever destination lie within that great door where
they entered and disappeared.

ON A WALL

It was fine to have eight legs when I was a Granddaddy
Long-Legs. I could travel very fast across our concrete
porch, and walk straight up our cinderblock wall with-
out falling. Others of my kind were up there and, O, we
would find one another and tangle our 16 legs, or 24 legs,
or 32 and rest very long. It was fine to be a Granddaddy
Long-Legs.

SAD POSSUM

It was hard being a possum.
I lived in a stone heap
and had to creep out
in the half light.

I didn't like to be seen with my bald,
narrow tail and hunched-up back.

And no one liked to see me
except cars in their headlights
who would like to hit me
and did.

SLEEPY SERPENT

. . . then my life as a black snake really got good when
with my wiggling tongue I smelled my way inside the
nursery of a farmer's chicks—all of them huddled under
a heat lamp . . . enough food for a Monday, a Tuesday,
a Wednesday when I stretched out under the heat lamp
with three lumps down my length. What a good sleep!
Then the chicken farmer came in . . .

NIGHT-LIFER

The world seemed all a-whirl
as I flew around a street lamp.

Night life made me dizzy
and I had to stop awhile and idle the motor.
My elegant designer wings
would quiver to a blur, then

off again—carried on reckless spins
scattering wing dust
with glee—flash-happy
as one abandoned to a spiral of sin.

MY MAD LIFE AS A BAT

My nights as a bat were hysterical. I flitted about like a druggy screaming echoes at the dark, like a murdered soprano, and I devoured every bloody mosquito right and left. Ones fat with human blood tasted best, and my stealthy cousins made that their specialty, grew long fangs and stole into bedrooms.

With humans ours was a love/hate story. They would chase me with brooms, ignoring all the mosquito bites I had saved them. Thanks to holy Church we had sanctuary in the belfries, and we would literally hang out there all day. Wingless rodents scurried beneath the rat cellar, but our lofty life was cerebral.

Our intriguing, sinister ways became so popular they made comic books and movies about a certain man who envied the ways of bats, and strove to serve justice outside the law. A noble madness indeed, far truer to our kind than the vulgar, commonplace expression "she has bats in her belfry."

To (the bat's) adroit Creator
ascribe no less the praise—
beneficent, believe me,
his eccentricities—　　　　*(Emily Dickinson)*

Uncollected Haiku

Winds scuttle about
whisp'ring here, whisp'ring there
spreading scuttlebutt.

He chewed tree branch off,
ate fresh berries where it dropped
—pretty smart squirrel!

Spring breezes sighed in
listening cedars, sowing
southern love stories.

Sun does not rise. No.
Horizon lowers brow in
slow adoration.

O be just a bee!
sweet singer whose fearless hum
comes with a stinger.

Jesus, love crazy,
what a queer, screwy, fickle mob
of friends you have!

When a kid, Jesus
would run on water—paid it
no mind. In his teens
he'd go out in wind
when waves were really whipped up—
now that was a blast!

Where went great circus
of summer's sounds? Folded up,
colorful tent—gone.

Dewdrop rolled off roof,
flashed in moonlight and tapped
one dry, withered leaf.

Fuzzy waning moon—
an old mind gone somewhat lost,
adrift, forgetful.

Lumbering school bus
swiftly speeds through dark flashing—
angel on patrol.

Small Chipping Sparrow—
Hear him chip persistently
time's hard, uncarved block.

First came thought—old, sour,
then growing complaints—thunder
growling at distance.

Each snowflake descends
with some secret whispering
soft intimacies.

Angel—golden hinge
swung on silver, silent bolt
opened gate of truth.

Night rains subsided
from slow, quiet palaver,
awaited morning.

Ice crunch under tires
slows to a stop, lights go out,
door softly thumps closed.

With quiv'ring wattle
Turkey quibbles with neighbors
in petty quarrel.

Cow, no longer mute,
bellows to relieve life's long
ache of existence.

Sun, with tawny mien
paces morning horizon
with soft, soundless paws.

Birds snick back and forth
with earliest hint of day:
Wake up little jerk!

Nothing about me
is quite so flawless as my
perfectionism.
Nothing is so warped
as my stubborn resistance
to showing my warps.
Nothing's so normal
as my sovereign disdain
for looking normal.

Does the flying bird
Sing? Or is the bird a song
that glides where it will?

BELLS OF THE HOURS

2014

CHRISTMAS MORNING

Tolling bells walked us through hallowed hours
while sun and I kept leisured pace with time,
as though by courtesy of bells we claim
time as ours. Light itself was washed by rain

on Christmas eve. Time, heedlessly, neglects
its vastness—steps serene to measured tolls.
Space, swollen to full, sways as one elect,
at tilt of bell, with sun and monks to stroll.

ST. AGATHA,
4 DEGREES FAHRENHEIT

On days this cold, the bell strikes
tight, indrawn, subdued. Swings
liquid and free on summer days.

Formed from molten flow, once
cast and chilled in mold, its voice
released upon this February freeze.

Agatha, saint of fire and foundries—
her frail relic, an uplifted veil, stopped
volcanic flow on a village street.

Some burning star reduced gases
to inert iron, exploded and flung
raw matter now refined to
this clapper, bolt, and dome,
which strikes, lifts and unfurls
veils of music on frigid air—

rigid iron transformed to sound
and finally forged to prayer.

BURIED FLAME

O living flame of love
That tenderly wounds my soul
In the deepest center!
St. John of the Cross

In early half-dark
I pass a smoldering source
of stale smoke smelled

a half mile away—
fuming, room-sized volcano
nearing extinction.

Dry, heaped-up trash wood
of buried intensity
burning all night long,

one spark on the ground.
I ignore it and walk by—
nothing there to see,

all smoke, smothered heat,
pale clouds wafting from the core
that took all this while

to hide its fierceness.
Its quiet intensity
returns each wood mote

to the universe.

Since now you are not oppressive,
now consummate! If you will.

ELEGY

for Fr. Chrysognous

Bell strokes telling time,
casually fall over retaining wall,
and lazily spill through the valley
entangled in their echoes.

Low sun stretched aslant
long shadows on November grass
empty staff lines of some melody,
never sung,
waiting for its notes.

None will come now.

A life has passed that made
notes enough for seasons full—
and then some.

This empty time stands quieted of
sounds departed.

Yet lingers still a subtle tangle,
an echo come
from what immortal hills?

LITTLE SCRIBE

Each instant at my desk
lays down an unwritten line
in some psalm undisclosed
—the quill and scrape
on parchment, rough on my palm,
the faint click of a latch far
down the hall, and silent lamplight
watches on.

A moment to go, or two,
and the bell will tell me
the spell has broken and shall
cast itself larger in choir.

The instant, suddenly shortened by half
precludes me writing more—O,

fear not, little scribe,
obedient, distressed,
you'll return to the rune
left off on the page,
its uncompleted *O*
gilded with silence.

Precious the gap
that arrests the line
from circling to a close

the curve suspended

from completion in time

where every instant,

its circumference hesitates,

breathless, to complete,

its script

in the timeless.

*A legendary medieval monk was a scribe, diligent for his work
and for obedience. When the signal for the Divine Office rang,
he immediately laid down his pen before finishing the illuminated
letter. When he returned, he found the letter was completed in gold
by an angel. In Zen calligraphy when a circle is drawn, the brush
is lifted before closing the form.

THE GREAT BELL

Beneath darkened eaves
all busy with twitter,
swallows anticipate

light enough to fly,
quite beside themselves with
excitement 'til the great

bell's torque, rock and iron clang,
imperiously rounded
the cloister court which trapped,

turned and intensified
sound up the late chilled night
where angels distracted

with timeless things were rung
down to join monks and swallows
in the timely work of

inviting in the dawn.

MERTON'S NOVICES: LATE 1950s

Young men came
looking for
     —don't know what—
Left the place
looking for
     —don't know what—
Of these I had no regrets.

Some came, seemed like
     looking—
heard some talk about
     —what—
     stayed awhile
and left
talking like— Well,—
     like somewhat.

Serious young men came looking.
took up talk about,
     —don't know what,
stayed long and left
talking
about everything what-not.

Some came completely
clear and sure about
     what—
Those I sent away.

Silent young men, a few,
came looking for—
        don't know what-
        stayed
and kept on looking
        stayed and never got to
        what—
wore out,
died,
had never stopped looking for
        what—
For these I have no regrets.

All of these I loved, but
seems the part I loved the best
was—
        don't know what—

TUG BELL

With slow, even pace through darkness
Angelus Bell tugs,

weighty with mystery,
steady as a barge
hauled into night harbor.

Three strokes in a row
repeated three times,
daily morning, noon, eve

bearing imponderable freight

one minute Seed

weightlessly deposited
in the silent moment

the Word itself Incarnate.

When tolling ceased
ringing resumed
with quickened speed

its load unburdened
the tug takes leave

to fetch a distant
treasure lobe.

PRACTICAL BELL

Our burial ground fills
with practical sounds
from Tierce bell,
drenching its dumb
unheeding crosses.

Alone I skirt around
this rim of destiny

stirred by the bell
to occupation
but only awhile

'til some day I'm left un-busied
in this ground's
silent keep.

DAY OF THE DEPARTED

Sext bell
softly merges
with stray echoes
in tones muted
for this Day of All Souls.

For these, the departed, we pray
while they offer us presence
too subtle to be felt.

And as we raise our suffrage
on their behalf,
they, pained at our grief, offer that
as their suffrage in return.

ST. LUCY'S NIGHT

A maze of branch shadows on ground
and walls cages me round—
thick bars, under looming guard
of winter naked trees—

the moon full, impossibly bright
—un-caged.

The bell for Lauds descends
through dark web of branches
in tones of kindness

as though to say: Your cage,
how illusory!

a shadow of your blindness
to your own intact, lucid,
and inescapable freedom.

St. Lucy was an early Roman virgin-martyr, imprisoned at the Coliseum.

UTILITY DOOR

The ever-dutiful door groans
with world weariness,
behind me closing
        slows and thumps to
conclusion—

to closed opinions
shut in on itself
while the busy world ignores it

until the next monk,
obliging himself,
opens wide, swings
and releases it
again
to its old

world-weary groan.

FEAST OF ST JOHN LATERAN'S BASILICA

A no-uncertain November cold
sets greyish on the Kentucky air.
Locust leaves shuffle
underfoot, sighing
lowly as straw. Slow as
a ghost I pace the court,
awaiting the bell for Lauds.

Monks, white sheeted in Cowls, pass
through with purposeful steps that
wraiths—uncertain—lack.

Bell strokes drop liquidly
into silence deeply pooled,
and soundly implore
a gathering of hearts.

Monks attend familiarly
at doors held open
as of guests welcomed
at a house that's a
faint reminder
of a house older still, sacred and distant,
itself a ghost of the further home
not made by human hands, where
a no-uncertain warmth ever
sets upon the season.

St. John Lateran is the oldest cathedral in Rome.

ELEGY

for Br. Thaddeus

Bier returned from grave,
Vacated surface rumpled,
eased by subtraction.

Cloisters ponderous
with lingering removal,
one stepping stone

gone, where foot remembers one.
Slowly now must grow
familiarity with

pothole of absence.
Retraction of face
insinuates displacement

of my secure place.

IMPENDING RAIN

Noting well, in measured code
with even, metered strokes,
the bell, sedate and careful, posts
announcement: time is grey.

The yard was prim, orderly, staid,
three grackles chased a crow away
to make the homestead safe.

A mockingbird made smart remarks,
some neighbor made reply,
banter was softly set aside
for hint of looming change.

A sheltering stillness hangs.
Two shrubs in leaf and blossom stand
white as girls, polite and good,
respectful of the worried nun

suspicious showers soon may come.
Earth and sky held their breath
when notice rang abroad,
in blunt, methodical code,

that called to children growing bored:
this blank and featureless day,

Time, so slow, will wash away.

JOHN THE EVANGELIST, DEC. 27

One bold light at stair-top
shines raw from high window
into a dark courtyard, damp
with thaw and moldering leaves—

this world of bald contrasts
John wrote of—one light brilliant,
all else dimmed, illegible.

One bell tells, retells one word
—all else overstated
and absurd:

life is simple: simply love.
A child knows this and once a child was
Love made flesh.

Each leaf loosened in this world
yields rich scent of this one Book.

DRAGON TRAINER

for Br. Rene

Late in Epiphany night
my sleeping-porch was disturbed
by lights approaching and a motor groan
creeping around the curve
to the propane tank.

The high cab nosed past,
a gem-lit dragon prince,
tentative and uncertain of his prey,
his endless chrome length
dotted with amber foot lights.
He stopped and released an anguished brake fart.

I curled deeper in my bag, sleepless,
un-stirring as a naked larva
in a cocoon that might easily be
swallowed in a single gulp.

The passenger emerged into the headlights,
a rickety, bent monk on a cane,
a shepherd, humble and meek,
to lead the dragon in tow,
tamed and polite and slow before
such fearless simplicity.

OKTOBERFEST

Red-green cypresses,
last troop of revelers drunk
Oktoberfest gone.

Indefatigable
clowns still milling around town
basked in golden sun.

Other trees wasted,
costumed hills charred to drab ash
exhausted all fun

yet these big boys are not done.

BELLS OF THE HOURS

(Verdin Bell Castings with names embossed:
St. Mary, large bell; St. Raphael, medium; St. Gabriel, small)

Dun air hangs with
fine spray that dries on my brow.
Archangel Raphael, stirred up from
distant memory of demon-battles, lifts,
strikes and sustains a tone

of sincerity laid heavily upon
this double-minded monk

alone in the dark who steps into
the awful room, for the unbearable
intimacy with God.

Choir stalls soon fill, brighten,
and psalmody begins to flow.
I push off onto its current
tossing up

> *. . . distress . . .*
> *. . . shortness of life . . .*
> *. . . shine on our children . . .*

That troubled expanse finally crossed,
I looked back—
None of that was about me alone.

Tierce bell, its mother-touch
strokes a tone that softly soaks
into grass and firs.

Urged so, I enter on
the foot-worried floor
crossed by minds
bent on toils already
crowding the day. Many
pebbles make the floor,
the floor by pebbles made

> *... I abide a stranger ...*
> *... my eyes to the mountains ...*
> *... standing within your gates ...*

Dove ponders refrain:
Gone there, gone there—how I am here!

Under noon's
high booming sun
the small, neutral bell for Sext
scuttles me to shadeless
space, its spare rank,
a survivor guard

> *... pressed me hard ...*
> *... who could survive ...*
> *... my heart's not proud ...*

Shall all be well?
Were all manner of things well?
Is anything well?
... very well
    ... well ...

Severe cicadas keep the heated world turning.

None's bell
squeezed small
by rush and talk
heard by some
heeded by none is
Gabriel's tranquil call

> *... in vain do its builders labor ...*
> *... I'll give no sleep to my eyes ...*
> *... it seemed like a dream ...*

Psalms nearly done, I notice at last I'm doing.

In high smooth curves
long winged birds turn
without a flap
    on distant watch.

Vesper's bell dimly
probes its thin
finger down between
sinks and showers
towels and socks.

Faintly tugs one up
from ground floor
through cloister funnel
to door swung large
on sunlit walls and
clarity resounding.

> *. . . heavens proclaim . . .*
> *. . . utmost bounds . . .*
> *. . . walk all round it . . .*

Groundhog, raised on his haunches,
gazes around.

Compline's ring:
clarification, clarification,
eases a way into
shaded grove of monks standing.

> *. . . in the shadow of your wings . . .*
> *. . . the plague that prowls in the darkness . . .*
> *. . . with length of life I will content him . . .*

Angelus tolls for you,
banished child,
returned,
returned to clemency.

Big St. Mary bell's
rings all wrested
from its belly
rocks to a halt,
done

all be rested
frets be-gone
done

monk
        be done.

3:00 a.m.

Ever-wakeful Vigil bell
spreads the silent air with unsleep,
carries round to walls and barns
which smoothes to a stream
that sets coyote howling
and monks to prayer.

Father Sacristan bursts upon
the darkened church, bustles
loudly, clearing his throat,
enough to evict demons
from shadows and corners.

> *... tear out their fangs ...*
> *... they gabble open-mouthed ...*
> *... our daughters graceful as columns ...*

—awake, wide awake once more—
all these histories—God's own dreams and nightmares—
sung.

AFTERNOONS
WITH EMILY

2011

MY LAST POEM

When I write my last poem
it will not say good-bye
to poetry, but hello to itself,

will heave a glad sigh
it got into the world
before the door closed,

will look to its companion poems,
that it might have place
among these orphans,

that they might reach out hands
in company to go together
into oblivion or into memory,

or to some secret cove
where eternity sits,
from time to time, and reads.

RESTLESS SILENCE

The enclosure wall runs the field,
ducks behind some pines
skirts the forest, dips and rises,
gently drops, then disappears.

Beyond, I can hear snow
melting in the woods.

What am I waiting for?
What enlightenment is in the sun
reflecting off the icy lake,
wearing it to a thin slick?

Dry grass in the wet field
is dusty with sunlight.
What is the grass waiting for?

A pigeon leaves a tree for another tree.

I can hear the sun
grazing the dusty grass,
until a breeze interrupts briefly
then settles for . . . a something . . .

Was it here already and gone?
Or was it only here
so I would come and wait?

Why this sadness when,
yielding to restlessness,
I rise and abandon what
never knows abandonment?

HIKER'S GUIDE TO THE MONASTERY KNOBS

In case you're lost:
Streams go down.
Follow that.

Upward trails go
towards the sun.—
Follow that.

Old trail leads
to a lost colony
of Mayapples.

In parts unknown
inhabited by
redbud and dogwood—
trust these familiar friends.

Budding beeches
dismiss dry leaves to
wind in conversation with time,

puzzling over seasons
past and present
forgetting which is which.

HOODED SENTINELS

Venus stood bright above the court
in darkness awaiting
the tolling for Lauds, which
carried forth clear as
a cadet-angel's voice.

The cloister's darkened windows,
tall as hooded sentinels, stood
hollowed out by long
hallowed strokes of
eternity's bell, that
swayed to a stop so
time could resume and
Lauds another day begin.

MARSH HAWK

The Marsh Hawk slow-meanders
not far above the ground.
He tilts, and sways, and wanders
and cares not where he's found.

The thought he had he loses,
and wonders what he meant.
So casually he cruises
to follow where it went.

Along the lazy hills
he sees if all is still.
And if it isn't that,
beware some sorry rat!

MAD MONK TO A NEIGHBOR
WHO LOST HIS DOG

Your dog is not lost, sir.

She is losing you and is out
cheerfully following her nose
where she can be just a dog
awhile, without interference
of being your pet.

Home is for two-footers
and she can very well find you
from anywhere 20 miles around.

If she's worth anything
she'll remember you're
in hell—lost, and she'll soon
come loping back.

DOG-STAR SKY

Under the Dog-
Star, one coyote
howled, stopped,
set off a pack
of yaps that tattered
night, its height
of glee gone
painful!

Misfits wailing
native claim,
frazzled me
spine to brain,
so alien I
underneath the
Dog-Star sky.

AWAKENINGS

Webs of clouds weave dreams
across the face of the moon
—sleeping, half smiling.

Muffled lowing of a cow
sends mother-comfort to
the hermit asleep
under the drifting moon.

"Strangeness! Strangeness!"
The owl cries
to the frosted world.

"That's a howling dog."
The monk awakened says.
"Strangeness! Strangeness!"
He goes back to sleep.

Nighttime troubadours
circle through woods and fields
—hounds singing hound love.

A mule cries out:
"I . . . I am the only mule!"
Then from a distance
another mule cries:
"I am the only mule . . . I!"
Night once more goes mute.

Webs of clouds weave dreams
across the drifting moon—
sleeping, half smiling.

HERMIT'S YARD

Sleek grackles slink
past black
one stretched neck
oil-slicked blue
checked out
this dude

dead set
one white-ringed
eye on him judged
him one dud

too wooden to slide
tip to tail
one slippery wave
sheer rhythm
high-step'n in grass
made smooth as wax
on jazz club floor

one up-beat leap
and off he flew
dropped behind
one white scat
to tell for me
that's enough of you

and for you O Hell
that's enough of that.

1 JULY

With its single note, single note
a common sparrow cleanses space
for meditation.

Its insistence convinces
of many tones ranging within,
within its ring.

At the core of a distant tree
a new sun, red and warm, hides
itself—heart of a sacred world.

Robins—exhilarated—circle, close
and part in greeting
of another, another summer day.

The sun leans along, earth traveler,
'til veils and mirages of clouds
disclose it had lifted

at a distance,
a distance far,

far after all.

CRICKET'S REVERIE

Summer now gone,
cricket's slow reverie
lingers on memory
of summer's song.

Less need be said
when things we said we'd do
were proved at last so few—
dreams left for dead.

Trees stand like harps,
strings bare just to the top
where golden notes hang caught
as song departs.

ANCIENT JADE

for Jacqueline Chew

Surrounded by music
she stands stable as
an ancient jade.

In her eye no gleam
more than a dim
sanctuary lamp,

for she is elsewhere,
where music roams
in sacred rooms

of ancient nostalgia.

NARCISSUS AGED

Lighted, rippled surface
caught his gaze in nets
of cross-hatch waves that
moved and stayed.

Its shimmering veil
suspended thought
'til breezes dropped.

The water-curtain smoothed
to mirror distant clouds in
vast lake of fathomless air.

He leaned down and caught a smile that
blossomed back—his face so small,
beneath such vastness—small.

FEAST OF ARCHANGELS

for Fr. Matthew Kelty

Resting in a motor chair at window,
no longer tramping open fields wading
where wind rolls waves of light and shadow,
his boredom aches at lawns cut flat and low.

Resting in a motor chair at window,
he asks Archangels, might there be a poem
strong enough to banish vicious mowers,
to justify each graceful blade that grows?

grand enough to open up broad visions
of grass returning tall from distant fields,
to stand in ranks and colorful divisions
on lawns from all banality now healed?

—where monsters of noise, exhaust, fumes, expense
flee clover, Bluegrass, Cone Flowers, Queen Anne's Lace?

ROOFLESS SOUND

What is this sound thinning
to a veil, older than
walkways and walls,
longer remaining
than any trees?

What's this cricket sound
this canopy lifted to night
filling the garden where trees
under stars lean and listen
year after year?

A roofless sound they sustain,
inhabit awhile and perish,
and after a season
occupy once again.

What then is this sound?

DAY WITHHOLDING

Some days the world holds off
at a distance, neither hot nor cold.
No promise is on the breeze,

birds converse elsewhere.

Heaven and earth—grey halves
of a closed shell, wherein I sit—
shriveled, loose nut, without
sap—some gnats, newly hatched

dance in my face, the only visitors
who like my smell and meager warmth.
Today, O let them have their way.

FADING MEDITATION

I grasped at consciousness,
thought led me down,
my head went numb,
snatched to non-consciousness.

Thought sunk me, 'til half spent.
I went opaque,
then pulled awake,
confused, what thinking meant.

Strange, that old instruction:
"Follow your breath."
For God's sake, breath!
What else's left for this one!

Lost like a cork at sea,
there, where I am,
is where I am,
all by necessity.

What's this? Loss? or sheer bliss?
What's your notion
of the ocean?
What place could better this?

WISE, UNWISE, OR OTHERWISE

Some
virgins
brought
lamps
with-
out
oil.

Some,
oil
with
lamp.

With
nei-
ther
oil
nor
lamp

I'm
Bride

TERESA AND JOHN

Nuns of Avila misunderstood
and reported that Teresa and John,
in conversation about things eternal,
had levitated above their chairs.

But their perception had gone askew.

For the two, steadied in Love Unmovable,
had remained fixed, and the chairs, the room,
and the turning world had dropped aslant,
as they're wont to do.

THE MISSING PEBBLE

for Fr. Louis Merton

On the pebble floor in the Chapter Room
one stone is missing.
Near the door, a char-hole remains
where a thunderbolt,
entered, struck, and removed
one rock only.

Forty years that hole remains,
the absent stone, un-replaced—
never seen again.

That same year the stone
was rendered electric,
a man, elected to be found
among monks he called burnt men,
was sundered electrically.

That precise wound
in the Chapter remains
a stigmata of absence
unnoted by monks
daily walking through.

TASK ASSIGNMENTS FOR GUARDIAN ANGELS

commissioned by Fr. Matthew Kelty

For the Food Angel

At my last meal on earth
no square fish without bones—a fish please,
    with tail and head and an eye
    that looks dead. No round flat salmon
    or a frozen uniform-cut with bread crumbs for scales.

potatoes with a skin, not flakes, pearls, or powder
    watered and stirred, from a bag, box, can.

beets or carrots with tops, that grew under sunlight.

eggs cooked fresh out of a shell, not a wax carton,
    or precooked, folded and frozen all in identical size.

lemonade from a lemon not powder,
    no wine-cooler, but one
    fermented to a finish.

For the Mortuary Angel

Let me be buried in my own body, not:

half of me bled down a sewer

the rest filled with a chemical, to make me look
        pink, un-dead, prepackaged and odorless.

Once I'm washed, clothed, lay me in church amid
        mummer of psalms, not in a mortician's vault with hours
        of chiller whine.

If needs be, use incense of a sacred air, not talcum-and-soap smoke.

Be the burial Christian, where death is real,
        not disguised, sanitized, Egyptian and pagan.

For the Angel of Passage

Carry me away as a mango moon
        in shaggy clouds to the west.

CONFESSIONS OF A DEAD-BEAT MONK

Of course, I've sat the same bench
brushing off flies and thoughts,
how many years? What winters of
silence and summer variations,

what prodigious mockingbirds
I've heard! And that kitchen job!
Broccoli and spuds on Mondays,
rice twice a week, and Oh,

toasted cheese sandwiches,
Fridays! This diet of psalms,
fifty and hundred, runs ever
on from bitter to sweet,

returns like the sun to bow
and stand. And I tread the same
stairs and stare at walls, blank
or lit rose and gold. I rise

with whippoorwills singing
at 3, though night ever keeps
its secret from me, 'til in
its treasure I'm locked.

Then I will be what always
has been, that enigma of
sameness between
now and the then.

MONKSWEAR

2008

THE COWL

–solemn as chant,
one sweep of fabric
from head to foot.

Cowls hanging
on a row of pegs–
tall disembodied spirits
holding shadows
deep in the folds
waiting for light,
for light to shift
waiting for a bell
for the reach of my hand
to spread out the slow
wings, release the
shadows and envelope my
prayer-hungry body
with light.

CINCTURE

a careworn strip of leather
circling round my waist
and drooping off my left hip
half way to the floor.

The trailer splits double:
a forked tongue
of the serpent that
never left us.
It rides my hips
and clutches my guts
until the grave swallows
us both.

One of seven
knot-lumps holds the belt-
slit fast, that slips
outward or in
as the body swells
or withers with
creeping mortality.

This hide strip of one dead cow
still yields with every breath I take
of sweet-stink from
a distant herd
heaving out loud complaints
of relentless desire.

Fossils of cattle longing
creep in every cell
belting my waist and
plunge off my hip to
reach the ground never,
ever to dangle
a swaying tail
a ceaseless twitch
that sinks to my quick
until the day I am
unquickened.

I retire at night
and with one easy sweep
I unfasten and hang
limp the old one-eyed trooper
on a hook

      for the night

until rising in the dark
and taking a breath
I hitch him back on
and stride off again
to Vigils.

ASH WEDNESDAY

A coal black char-cross,
is generously smeared
on each shaved head
front to back, side to side
—no subtlety about it.

Remember, Paul,
you are coal dust . . .
back home in coal country
soot in the air,
caked up nostrils
lodged under fingernails.

Kids, don't track up,
don't go near the coal bin.
Dad made sure of that,
painted a Devil on
the coal-bin door.

We heard Jews were
shoveled into a furnace.
We heard: Be good
or the Devil will put you
into the furnace.

My big brothers invited
my twin sister and I
down to see the devil.
I quietly descended behind her.
Just when she saw it, I yelled
clutched her shoulders and
she began to cry

terribly.

Even into adult years she would
blame me about that. Who knows?
perhaps she *did* see the Devil.

Remember, Paul,
you are ash
and ashes are
no joke.

DAD'S ASH TRAY

*God's image remains within you
even though you superimpose upon it
the earthly likeness of the man of dust . . .*
ORIGIN

Round brass rim with black char in the middle,
the only shiny thing in the living room.

Dusty golden with three notches in it,
a smudge in the middle, rough to the touch.
Afterwards my fingers did not taste good.

It arrived as a gift
from Dad's office,
pure gold maybe, or as good as.
A surprise gift.
In the center, I saw my face golden.
My twin too saw my face,
but I did not see hers.
How come? A magic bowl.

Then he spoiled it
knocked his pipe down against the shiny tray
and left all that blackness.

In my infant curiosity
I went to find my face
touched the tarnished rim
and dumped ashes on the carpet.

I was told not to touch it again,
the only shiny thing in the room.
Then my hand was roughly wiped clean.

Why anyone would want
to keep ashes I did not understand.
You couldn't eat them.

If you scrub it hard, my brother says,
it'll be shiny gold again.
Scrub hard. No one does.

It sits, a sallow gold frame
around an opaque mirror.
So it stays that way.

My twin and I, old enough to walk,
were put in the play pen for nap time,
with some boring toys
good for nothing but for throwing outside the pen.

Then she cried and said she wanted Dolly here.
So repentant, I devised to climb
for the very first time ever,
over the wooden pen bars,
brought the toy back, and climbed back in.

Then I saw the ash tray—the golden dish,
the one shiny irresistible thing in the room.
And no one in the room but us two . . .

MONK'S CASSOCK

I stand a man of the cloth
—and plenty of it—
hidden inside a steam-pressed
cotton tunic snappered up
to a prim collar which stands
one inch high
—sanitary, bloodless
washable, white for me
washed clean in
the blood of the Lamb—
a pretty pricey item!

On either side
pockets of inexhaustible depth.
Magic pockets!
I have to lean sideways
to reach bottom.
Contents on the right:
handkerchief, penlight,
Swiss Army knife,
chapping lotion,
pitch pipe, rosary.
Left side: keys, dental
floss, notes to be
discarded, eyeglasses.
Pockets deep enough
to smuggle two wine bottles
right through the cloister.

PRIMAL PRAYER

Bombs fall in Bagdad.
Bombs fall.

A child dies in Bagdad,
another child is born.
Bombs fall and explode.
Another child is born
and dies.

I cannot say yes,
I cannot say no.
Would I only have the voice of an infant
I would cry, I would wail.
Only my infant wail
would touch
Your Holiness.

Only the infant wail
is truth.

THE HOOD

—a hiding place
for the head

a portable anonymity

a refuge from
artificial light

a cover to make
dimness dimmer

to make time
slow down

to make ready
for the rain

for the rain that will come.

Under this thin
black fabric
I brood long
slow and steady

a yes,
an un-
qualified
yes

against that day
that downpour of
no

      no

  no
that will surely come

Then I will slip
my hood back and
let my old white head
shine with a
pure, unqualified

yes.

HOW MANY YEARS?

Visitors ask: how
long-a you been
here? I answer,
like some other
from elsewhere,
47 years.

But it is a fiction. Time has
shrunk not lengthened.
I used to live by month
and year. Now if I can bump
through just this week,
I'll leave time
for bells to keep,
and bear a moment
for all its worth.

But, sorry, a truckload of time
just came roaring in,
to empty, sort and stack.

How long have I been here?
Excuse me, I
haven't gotten here yet.

POSSESSED BY A HABIT

Sorry, but I can't seem to shed
this habit I'm so given over to,
this monkwear, this second skin
I'm so habituated to.

I've worn it 'til the habit has
worn me quite down
to a shadow of the man
I once was. You would
hardly recognize the boy
who at least had *some* promise
and risked talents, life, and
opportunities for the sake
of a possessive, chronic
habit which he won't shake off,
that holds him so hide-bound
he has all but lost
everything

which seems to be
the way he wants it
given the merry way
he carries on with
no thought of past,
future, or of what
might become of him

once he wakes up
and finds himself without
means or ability
to sustain so religiously
his mystifying
habit!

Just you see—unless
he quits this habit it will eventually
carry him to the grave.

Amen, Alleluia!

HAIR-CUTTING DAY IN AN EIGHTEENTH CENTURY SILVER-POINT

Hair-cutting comes once a month
according to the Book of Usages, everyone
gets shaved on the same day.

Three monks sit attended by
two Laybrothers and one Choir Monk.
A novice waits nearby reading a book,
with his hood up against air
coming through a half-open window.
His cold feet hug one another.
He wears wooden shoes with
up-turned toes, as do the others.
A large key dangles from his belt strap,
for even in monasteries
a door must be locked.

One burly barber with a blacksmith's paw
delicately supports a flat razor with
his little finger. His speechless lips sag,
he gazes pensively down his massive nose
attending to the almost sleeping head
of a white-bearded one,
with fingers interlocked on his lap.

Beside him, with hands placidly folded,
a Brother rests with his thoughts,
lips a thin down-curved line
as he, perhaps, appraises a crop failure.
His dark half-bald head
is guided lightly by the priest,
whose own side fringes
remain to be cut.

A frail senior sits with infinite patience,
head tilted slightly, face worn sensitive
to every whiff of sin and infidelity
in God's precious garden.

Down the shadowed stairway
descends a Brother with book in tow.
Up on the wall hangs a small shrine
of some hooded saint who
stretches compassionate hands
down to this quiet brood of
the blessedly mournful.

MY SCAPULAR

Dark crow wings
two black swatches
front and back
stretched down
over head, heart,
belly, to just below
the knees.

A crow never migrates.
He hangs around all winter,
hollers at the cold
and flaps off to where
the rest of the gang
is making enough of a ruckus
to kill off winter
'til spring seeps in.

A "murder" of crows
they're called.

Every day I lift and
drop over my head
this flutter of
black fabric
and hurry off
to crowd in
the echoic choir

where enough of a
row is made
to melt the icy core
belted beneath
my scapular chanting
in its rough
heated crow way

Nevermore,
icy core

Nevermore

Nevermore.

SCAPULARS

White robe
black stripe:
monks

Black fur
white stripe:
skunks

From both
best to keep
your distance.

DONNING THE COWL

is like fighting a sail
made of 4 yards of cotton.

My first try:
hold collar with one hand
with other hand
gather hem
up to neck
swing it round
over head and
drop-release
over body
in one
flop.

Bad try! I'm
smothered and blinded.

Improved method:
Gather hem to collar,
first fit around neck
then drop-release the rest.
Punch out long, impossibly
long billowy sleeves.
Then with nifty flick
of wrists heft up
excess cloth

clear your hands
lower hood, straighten tip
with arm in Full Nelson
twist behind.

Then briskly step
to the next
prayer-attack on
God in church.

MY LONG TAIL

What is the significance of . . . ?

Inevitably visitors ask
about the long tail on my belt
a yard of superfluous leather.
They sometimes think
I am the Abbot because
my tail is so long, or I'm
advanced in status,
someone enlightened.

My utilitarian answer:
it's something obsolete.
It could hitch the cowl
behind the back while
washing hands or making a bed.
No one, anymore,
would make a bed in their cowl,
or even, maybe, make their bed.

I am a vanishing species
with a dangerous tail
apt to get caught in the car door,
a Doberman they didn't dock,
a horse like John Henry whose
14 foot of tail fit his fame for arrogance.
I stride with tail swinging free

annoying the practical-minded
in their mail-order belts
who believe in nothing insignificant.

My significance is
I am no more significant
than neck ties or coat lapels
or studs on a belt.
In an age where hat or shirt is
a walking billboard
for Nike or Bud Light
I reserve the privilege
to be a mountain ram with
a head of French Horns
a puffin with axe-head beak
a peacock trailing a Persian carpet
I remain a freak of natural excess,
a side track of evolution,
a question for the archeologist
of the human dig who
will pick me up, look me over
and fail to figure out:
What's the significance of that?

STRAW MATTRESS

A sturdy duck-cloth case
was tightly stuffed, sealed,
punctured, and buttoned flat—
a unique smell of straw
and flax, a few seeds caught
in the weave. When sat on
it yielded a muffled crunch
but little comfort. In a year it
sank to the shape of the body.

Every autumn mattresses were
lugged outside to air out sweat,
returned and flipped over
to its flatter side. Mine was
second-hand, had dips and peaks
in the wrong places, as if
I must conform to the shape
of an anonymous someone,
conform to any monk through
years of living together
always, in the church, scriptorium,
refectory, fields, Grand Parlor,
shaped, punched, re-shaped,
softened to a dough—until
you find your own hard bones
that will make someone else yield.

In these latter days, I sleep under
the open sky as my dormitory,
shaping myself to every new
climate and constellation as
the year moves on—waking face
to face with Hercules, Leo, Orion,
each one aloof, silent, each an enigma
making its own ancient, anonymous imprint.

MOUNTAIN CLIMB

I set out alone towards the east,
walking in a summer afternoon
on a secret trail through
a grassy forgotten valley
and find my way to a mountain
that no one knows about.
I have been here before,
explored alone the route
that only I know. It is very familiar
though changed—
always familiar, though
never twice the same.
I have the energy
to take the long irregular climb.

I arrive at the summit
totally alone. Something absolute
grips my senses. I all but breathe it in.
I have been here, I know
I have been here before.

The descent glides past
a wooded meadow
to the monastery, where
I will be happy to show
it to others.

I awake.
It is dark.
My sense of the summit
begins to fade, as always.
But this time I will
help it stay.

I walk it in the dark.
Alone, after Lauds,
towards wintry hills,
distant silhouettes,
on the pale road confident
in the dream-memory,
—the summit beyond no more
than shadow and sky.

It is enough.

LAUGHTER
MY PURGATORY

2002

THAT TIME AT CANA

We thought it was a joke
—a kind of wicked joke—
just when spirits were high
and the vats low
I was supposed to
pour water into the goblets!

As good as telling everyone to go home.

"Do whatever he tells you,"
said the strange lady. . . .
The quiet young man
seemed as annoyed as I, at first.

But the boys and I got to laughing
—we couldn't help it—
and went ahead and just did whatever he told us.

Even the bridegroom seemed
in on it all:
when he tasted the cup
his eyes lit up!

After so much cheap wine
plain old water tastes so good!

But guests started gathering around . . .

It was too curious, and I stole a taste.
That's when the sobriety hit me.

I was afraid.

—didn't say anything.

The boys started talking.
Guests decided they had been drinking on the side
and had taken to telling stories.

Then I got blamed.
"It came straight out of the well," they said,
and the more they protested
the funnier it got,
Oh! what an evening—I thought there would
never be an end to it all.

To this day there hasn't been.

I tell you—
I would trade my soul
for one more taste of that drink:

its bouquet of paradise,
rich, full-bodied as blood,
subtle as that strange woman's smile,
exhilarating as the laughter of angels.

MEDITATION METHOD

Listening to a concert
   people sit
   very still.
The music speeds up
   we listen the more
   and sit
   very still.
The faster it goes,
   the less we move;
   the rhythm pulls tighter
   the lines move swifter,
   in legato ascends.
Holding tighter, I sit faster,
   break into
   double time, I hear the cello
   echo in counterpoint
   as I sit stiller
   and move faster.

A deaf man enters the room
   wonders at all the people
   there
   who are gone.
Nowhere gone, because
   they are there.
They sit and stare, and see not
   as though they were elsewhere;

Each moment might never end
  or any moment suddenly break
  into an avalanche—
  but does not.
They stay still
  and forget time is passing.
Time has forgotten them;
  is blind to heads leaning,
  sitting very still,
still as a nun before dawn
  forgetting the dark,
for this melody moves in light,
  banks and turns and dives;
a circle of swallows
  skating on air,
  leaving, returning,
  crossing the high arena,
blind to listeners sitting very still
  in the semi-dark of a concert hall.

The deaf man turns and leaves,
  senseless of how so many people
  are a single winged creature
  soaring on an updraft,
  cresting in golden air
  towards an unlimited horizon.

SNAPSHOTS OF MOM

She brushed her hair, bunched the strands
and tossed them out the window
for birds to make a nest.

Favorite swear word: "O Jerusalem!"

I asked what they were fighting about in World War I.
She gazed off with face blank, lifted her shoulders and
let them drop. I thought it was ignorance or something
completely beyond her. Since then I have read many
histories—I now regard it as wisdom.

Grey at 45, a tuft still black concealed at the nape of her neck:
"I had raven hair."

In High School she had to write a story and read it to the class:
"My story was about this girl who takes something from her
boy friend.
He tries to find it, and—Oh, I was so
embarrassed—all the boys laughed when I got to a line that
said: 'He crept into her room and searched through her
drawers' . . . "

Best meal: fried chicken, green beans, and mashed potatoes,
Sunday afternoons, invariably.

"What did the Reverend Monsignor say at Mass today?"
She replies:
"Whereas . . . of course . . . therefore . . . in so far as . . . "

Learning to drive at 52:
a car opposite makes a left and collides.
My brother out of the car and talking to the driver;
she behind the wheel, her foot still pressing the brake.

Returning home late at night, the end after months of
visits to
Dad in the hospital:
I hear calming voices,
hers rising above:
"I didn't want that to happen!
I didn't want that to happen!"

Settled in a new house, near relatives again:
My brother stops by on the way home from the coal
mine:
"How are you?"
She sits down on a stool: "Sometimes I can hardly keep
going."—I had thought everything was fine.

Friday nights sitting with Rachel in front of the TV, glasses of
beer in hand, watching the boxing matches, which
came after
I Remember Momma.

After school I found her sitting in a dark corner of the
church vestibule: "Are you all right?"
"I'm thinking of what to buy for Christmas while in
town."

To the Sodality ladies:
"I can always tell when my son is home from High
School—crash, bam, slam."

"The day your Aunt Katherine was married we carried
her down main street in Farmington in a wheelbarrel."

"Your Dad said the first time he saw me
he was on the jitney riding past home and saw me
coming down the front steps.
He said to himself:
'That's the girl I'm going to marry.'"

Driving through the country we come upon a hay field
being harvested.
"O, now that's what I consider really beautiful!"
—the windrows curving, dark and light along
the contours of the hills.

I, in my Trappist habit, speaking alone with her:
Her question left me speechless:
"Do you have faith?"

Another one of her children leaves the Church:
"What will she do?—out completely and left with nothing!"
—her upturned palm drops to the side.

Her first child died an infant.

"I believe Jacky went to heaven and became an angel."

—this over a cup of coffee at the kitchen table fifty

years later. She continued counting birthdays.

At 75, holding an infant when my Aunt arrives:

"Don't worry, Ethel, this one's not mine."

Always healthy until that terminal heart condition:

"I've never *had* anything before, only colds . . . and babies."

Last visit home:

"That garage down from the church burnt to the ground.

It used to be a chapel where your father and I were married."

Last phone call home, her voice much weaker.

I try to revive her with enthusiasm and interest.

She is swept back, loses the effort

—Aunt Frances takes the phone.

DREAMLESS SLEEP

Unsleeping I lay
outdoors in the grey of night.
The slightest ruffle
opens my eyes to the still
dark form of a fox,
alert, stopped in her tracks
by my two large eyes.

I'm not startled at her
so she is not startled at me,
but cautiously turns
and walks at her own quiet pace.

The night grows longer.
The moon sinks through
pearl-grey clouds
toward the dark mountain.
Sleep, at last, will be dreamless.

FOR EILEEN 1940–1995

I dream you are alive—
young, healthy, real as daylight.
We're in the garden.

I thought you were dead!
Why simulate death and leave?
Were you with some man?

She is mute, then says:
He is a kind of healer.
They say he once died.

My alarm wakes me
to dark. To reality's
hard, opaque, sad dream.

MY FIRST SIN

The half dome yard of my childhood home
slopes into blackness. Random
points of light move
and vanish in the air.
I'm told they are alive and
my sister names them for me.

And I think: How are lightning-bugs caused by lightning?

Here—they won't hurt you, hold it in your hand.

The spaces between my fingers light up a cool green
and disappear. Yet the thing does not go away
and lights another corner of my hand.

Let's catch and put them in a jar.

And the night becomes a wild dance of frustration
and random luck. The jelly jar
becomes not the loaded bank I wanted,
but does crowd with light when shaken once,
twice, but not a third or forth time.

See, if you tear it out the lighter stays lit.
You can smear it on your skin too.

When morning comes Mother asks:
What happened to the jar of lightning bugs last night?

We threw them into the commode, turned off the light,
flushed and they spinned around
faster and faster.

Oh honey, don't do that . . .

But it was pretty!

SKETCHES OF GRANDMOTHER

I

Saying little, she sits very still, listening. So frail, she sits
as the slightest movement of her frame begins, a rhythm
with the head nodding in assent, in the rate of the heart-
beat nodding, ceasing and beginning, continuing on,
nodding in assent to the world as it is.

How could so many hills and curves fit within one face?
as if the whole globe was there made small. One skin
feature prominent, round, is called, I'm told, a mole—
something that old people get. Named and so diagnosed,
it seemed an ordinary face after all.

At Grandmother's were copies of LIFE, with big pictures
from all around the world—big and puzzling, telling of
the war and things that came over the radio. Sometimes
pictures of "the firemen's parade" she called it, meaning
nudes on the ceiling of the Sistine. Meanwhile futiley I
searched back and forth for some kind of parade.

Alone on the porch she suddenly gives way to laughter,
repeated and prolonged, teasing and fussing, with no
company in view. I rush out the door in time to see a
chipmunk spin and disappear, afraid of me but not of her.

At the end of a visit, amidst good-byes, kisses, and smiles,
she projects towards the kids her false teeth. I take it

as a special grandmother's smile, bigger than the other
grown-ups if not very pretty.

Leaning over the porch railing at nightfall, a conversation
begins I've heard before. Aunt Madeline says to her:
"It's about time for you to go to bed."
"Well, don't forget to lock the door."
"Why should I lock the door?"
"A darkie might come in and carry me off."
"Listen to that! Eighty-two years old and still thinking
anyone would carry her off!"

Whenever my sister and I left the house to go downtown
—downtown was a whole block and a half long—we were
reminded:
"Don't let the darkies grab you."
I imagined that was some private boggy of hers—no one
in that town fit the description.

My oldest brother kneels by her chair with a camera:
"Can I take your picture Grandmother?"

II

Weeks later, the result:
She looks out astonished
delicate, poised
eyes deep and full
ancient yet timeless
astonished perhaps at her own offspring in the bloom of
manhood,

astonished at the world as it is.

In the same room a portrait of Pius XII,
erect, lean, looking out,
sitting as if forever, the white ermine
running vertical on the front of his red velvet coat,
sitting alert in a world where all is in revolution,
seated as if chaos did not exist, as Abraham Lincoln sat,
as Whistler's Mother,
as if there were no other reality than this frame on a wall
facing a portrait on the wall opposite
of the venerable Bishop in the seat of an obscure moun-
tain diocese, and between them
Anna Deveny Hagerty real and alive,
tending the house with her quiet,
where the noise of six children grown has withdrawn,
where noise will come of grandchildren, and children of
theirs;
her rosary nearby at rest
sitting with her thoughts, or with no thoughts
with no heaviness, nor lightness
not willing to be, nor not willing to be
as if no other activity were in creation,
and creation were this being
on this chair, in this room, in a house
on a hillside across from the Methodist Church
in a coal town in West Virginia.

Later I found the photograph in the trash.
"Mom, what is it doing here?"
"Oh, it makes her look so old . . . "

THE BOTTOM LINE IS . . .

I'll not stand for
how you always draw your bottom line
an inch above me.

I'm through towing the line
on a bottom that gets yanked out from under me
every time the bottom line of
everything you're above doing
becomes
the bottom line of everything I've already done.
Like you've kicked out the bottom and
there's no where to go but
down,
so low
not even Satan can draw
the line that is me
landed flat on my face
where you can walk all over me
and make ME your definition of

the bottom line.

ULTIMATE MORALITY

If I desire the cessation of desire,
I still desire. Trying hard
to end it all is still to try.

Tried by life, with pistol to my head,
I try back with
one last shot
and down I go, lost to being tried
by my own desire.

What illusory self began this desire
to end desire?
I canonize my craze for ultimate autonomy
by a kamikaze lunge,
offering everything to the idol of
the wanting I.

The Buddha never wanted nirvana.
Saints have quit the hell of wanting heaven.

A NIGHT VISITOR

A grey cloud cover
hides the moon, blanketing light
as night grows lonely.

My ears are stifled
by the crush of my own thoughts
'til silence says: Hush.

These ears are windows
Opening on quiet night
where my soul can breathe.

If I could reach out
to touch this fragile silence
she would shy away.

She offers presence,
not familiarity,
to my calloused hand.

Close as my own breath,
though my mind be far away,
precious as a prayer.

Rare is the moment
when, with nothing on my mind,
I hear her passage,

subtle as a sigh.

TERRORS
OF PARADISE

1996

UNQUIET VIGIL

Stale prayer from
unreal depths—
depths I assume are mine—

are relieved by
real sleep,
that awakens me to my

real shallows where
prayer amounts to
almost nothing
or less.

Such an infinity where
amost nothing
dividing endlessly
never reaches
nothing

wherein are
real depths
not mine . . .

Be kind.
Myself, to myself, be kind.

MOTHER OF TIME

In the middle of night there comes a pause
      when time goes to sleep.
If by grace, fortune or some feral instinct
      you should awake
you are nowhere between the time you went to sleep
      and the time you will wake up.

No use asking the clock for time gone to sleep
      and slipped off, leaving nothing
but this empty space where slow and fast
      cannot compete,
where before and after are unoriginate—
      no more than twins struggling
in the womb of sleeping mother who is

      you forgotten by yourself.

WINTER DAYBREAK

Were I not given ears
how could I hear this silence?
Without eyes, how see
this almost empty sky
with its broken fiction of clouds?

How hear the distant
hush of asphalt under rolling tires,
or see the awesome wings
of haunted clouds?

I thank You for ears
to hear this silence—
the bird that spoke before
I listened, swift sky-mote
falling in the dark and banking
into light, stirring up
the orange dawn.

The scratch of my thought runs
with the bark of a crow
who claims the horizon his,
and leaves the center for
me and all the civilized
freaks he avoids,
here where we crowd our ears with
the clank and quarrel of daily
work. For ears

that hear not Your silence, Lord,
O rebuke me;
with the twit-twit of
the titmouse at dawn.

SPRING RUMPUS

Rock and run a wrestler wind
wakes the resting trees for spring,
whips giant water tower legs,
brashly hums a hornet hum.

Creaks aging church roof rafters,
one by one old knuckles crack in
sturdy back of praying mother,
she don't mind her rampage kids—
winds young pass over every year.

Robber at my quaking window
shook my pretty room today,
snatched her tender breath
clean away.

Beware, beware! the old wall grumbles,
I'm in no mood to play.

MY SILENCE IS THE LORD

My silence is the Lord,
I listen, his silence speaks at all times.
When I listen not, my hearing is filled with words
and my tongue takes to rambling.

My resting place is the Lord
a hideaway on a mountain height.
The lonely seek and find him.

My resting place is the Lord,
a low valley by the runlet.
All humble steps lead there.

"Turn in to my place and sit quietly.
Drink from my stream and my vintage.
Cast off your shoes, discard your hardships
and listen to my evening song:

"I seek a heart that is simple.
With the peaceful I spread my tent.
I will wash your feet and dry them,
my silence will be their perfume.

"In your quiet steps I will follow.
None will know whence we come and where we go.
To the world you will be my silence,
in your passing they will hear me.

"In your absence I will be present.
Though you die, I Who Live am yours—
I live as yours forever."

ELEGY FOR BROTHER PACHOMIUS: GUESTMASTER

Slow shuffler with hang-dog face,
eyes looking up are marble shines.
Doctor Emeritus of flowers and
        culinary crafts,
turning a corner as if the walls move
        and you alone stay still.

That stocking cap covered a head
        from which nothing of the world was hidden.
In which all things swam in the mild season
        of a gentle vision: the harsh and heartless
        with the true and the pleasant.

And so guests came, mothers and uncles, kids and babies,
        birds and dogs, the news, the worries,
        the personal stories.
and were set at ease and made at home
        before any knew how or why.

As the year ends, and rain falls
        you lay down for a long, long nap—
and warm clouds scurry towards the north.

I go to my room and quietly close the door,
        catching a glimpse between here and reality
of your face, not grey but ruddy.

Eyes looking up are happiness shines.

WILD DOGS

Wild dogs on the horizon
howling in the darkness
souls of the lost
wandering, frightened,
braying out from the midst of . . .

fading off, returning
in the breeze, lost in my sleep
crying from by-gone valleys
beyond reach
howling on
forgotten.

No prayer for dark beasts in the wilderness.

RETURN OF THE OLD WATERTOWER

On the night breeze comes the odd ghost of a departed friend,
once conspicuous for his racket.
South winds no longer clatter and clank,
but whistle softly and fall silent.

Cranky old thing, ugly enough to stop a hurricane—
protective idol of yard buildings!
Straddle-legged, bossy, and steel-laced up to the hips,
holding aloft his own counsels:
they were beyond our reach, though our lives depended on it
when poured into our drinking cups.

Was that a spike on his helmet or crusader's cross?
—a fierce Quixote windmill fending off errant knights.
Sad how none were among these
soft-stepping monks.

Occasionally one monkeyed up
on his shoulder and waved at onlookers,
fixed metals, tightened belts,
and painted new armor on.

A lonely sentinel, his aloof neighbor was
a church steeple with whom he would
never reconcile.

One windless night he waited rusty and inert
as Dorothy's tin man, when the tool shed caught fire.
A bird's nest stifled in his siren horn,
bolted on like an ear gone deaf.
Tons of water held aloft, unused
because the fire truck wouldn't start.

I wake and November winds sweeping north
strike no auditory damage. Long gone, Old King Lear—
he might be found stupidly wandering a solitary tundra,
frozen water bursting from seams in his head,
icicles sprouting splendidly
from his ancient towering frame.

The following six nocturnes were written on successive days, in the same location, under a grand Ginko tree in a dark garden, with a small waterfall in the center; each at the same hour following Vigils, which itself is divided into two or three Nocturnes.

FIRST NOCTURNE

Dry Bliss
Only this half moon now
while this now is not yet eternity.

Only dusty veils rolling over the slow moon
while the All is yet unseen.

A frail trickle of water I hear,
only a sky cricket
while the unutterable is yet unsounded.

This silence is music unto itself,
but is my rarified purgatory,
scarcely mentioned in any poem,
to the catechism a closed book.

Nobody told me how to get here
or asks how long will I stay.

Strange mercy—this dry bliss,
which poets miss, the religious dismiss,
for the wordless and poor alone

so tender a kiss.

II NOCTURNE

A tenor dog punctures the dark horizon like a yard light.

Dark vines climb the pale garden wall
and mass their blackness with fir trees

where nests the cradle moon in deep crystal air
under the arching foliage of a black cherry tree.

Frail crickets linger on the threshold of silence.

Out in this cold air, warm with coffee inside,
a blanket of still air wraps itself around me
but does not nip.

Water, the constant water, echoes
round the enclosure walls.

Headlights creep past the wall slots—
A stranger departs from this nightbed of prayer

and another quietly arrives.

4:15 a.m.

Once again night.

Not until I quiet once again
to the cricket's song do I know
how many fathoms of noise
I have descended:

each strata humming with some restless shade,
sullen and territorial,
some stubborn rancor,
some muted, deflated desire,

until

at the murky bottom
a hole drops deeper into
an open sky of night air,
tiny insect sounds
and the distant bark of farm dogs.

ONE HOUSE

A starless sky, the ground featureless:
    one same earth where
Syria, Iraq, Egypt
    happen:
Same floor, same ceiling,
    one same
    house of God

So insufferable a place to sit,
    but sit I do.

THE WAYWARD MOON

The wayward moon
rumples up a confusion
of clouds around the sky.
Trees rise tall and bare,
a blue spruce surges
in dark billows to a point,
as hills roll under the limpid
touch of moonlight.

A dog somewhere off makes
distant argument, another
rebukes, while a third
yaps and warbles long
as a train down a valley.

But the careless moon
has no ear for quarrels.
Tomorrow the last shave
of shadow will fill
and she'll sail round
and clear of the random
netting, where stars are
snagged and lost, gems
scattered in a restless
bed chamber.

All these years I have worked
towards a certain life,
and now I have it.
Then why rankle so
over shades of inconsistency?

Tomorrow the moon will
sail round and clear
as the day of birth,
naked as the eye of Divinity.

III NOCTURNE

All fallen silent now, not a night creature sounds
        the stars rising up in chorus
        too immense to be heard,
most ancient of visible things.
        Yet the light is as young to itself
        as when it first left that star.

My sight is cleansed in its liquid light.

Perhaps the star burnt out eons ago,
        The light travels so far,
yet the light pours down
        ever as new, still young
when I am extinguished and long forgotten.